The *New* Glamour

Interiors with Star Quality

RIZZOLI
NEW YORK

New York Paris London Milan

JEFF ANDREWS

The New Glamour

Interiors with Star Quality

Written with Kathryn O'Shea-Evans
Photography by Grey Crawford
Foreword by Kaley Cuoco

I lovingly dedicate
this book to
Eleanor Mondale.

Contents

Foreword

full disclosure: I am *not* a writer. Not even close. I act out funny things that other people write. So when I was asked to write this foreword, I thought, How the hell can I do this? I don't write! All I know is that I have very strong feelings about everything, including Mr. Jeff Andrews. When I think of Jeff, I get a huge smile on my face, accompanied by a massive sigh of relief. This is how I've felt since the day we met.

The home I currently live in was originally designed and decorated by Jeff. I fell in love with the house, but also everything that came with it. The interior decoration, the furniture, the art—I wanted it all! I begged the previous owner to sell it to me. I ended up with many pieces, and I remember saying, "I *must* work with whoever decorated this house!" In came Jeff. We met, and it was love at first wallpaper. Does that make sense?

There was such a warmth, an ease, and a comfortable confidence about him. I instantly trusted him. Within one conversation, he understood my style, my personality, and, most importantly, my heart. This house meant everything to me, and he knew I wanted it to be perfect.

I told Jeff from day one, "I know you're the best at what you do. I want two options, max, of everything, and if I can't choose, just choose for me!" I don't think he believed I would actually be that way, but I was. I knew he would turn this house into a home, and he did. Since then, we have collaborated on many of my properties, including my riding barn, which he adorned with five massive chandeliers. When he told me his chandelier idea, I thought, Oh, God, I don't think that would work on a horse property! He said trust me, and I did. When I saw the chandeliers hung in the barn aisle, I almost fell over. It was and is the most gorgeous thing I have ever seen, and it continues to be the talk of anyone who sees it.

I love Jeff for so many reasons. His talent is beyond measure, but he is as grounded as they come. He thinks outside the box and designs for the specific client . . . with no ego or attitude ever.

I look around at the home he helped me create, and I think how grateful I am to have him in my corner. I can't wait to work together on many more projects in the future. He's stuck with me now, kinda like the Hermès horse wallpaper he hung in my kitchen—neither is going anywhere anytime soon.   *–Kaley Cuoco*

Introduction

Old Hollywood glamour has been etched in my mind for as long as I can remember . . . sweeping staircases, flowing drapes, chandeliers, wonderfully shaped furniture, and a feeling of extravagance and formality we rarely see today. That was the past, but the feeling of glamour in interiors has been transformed into what I call the *New* Glamour. Still as lovely and decadent as before, but on a modern and livable level that reflects the way we live now.

When I was growing up in Southern California, we moved around a lot. It forced me to be able to acclimate to new situations quickly and served as a catalyst for my burgeoning design mind. Even as a child, I reinvented every new room I had, whether it was arranging the furniture in different ways or turning magazine pages into artwork for my walls. Whenever we moved, my mind went whirring in a million different directions, absorbing everything visual at all times. I also loved to sing. At each new school I attended, I made a beeline for the choir room—I knew I would find genuine people there, and that it would feel like home. It was the one thing in my life that was a constant. Musical theater came next, and then I began to study dance . . . seriously. After much sweat and tears, I became a professional dancer, then eventually a choreographer, working internationally with sport companies like Puma, Reebok, Skechers, and Vans doing live performances at trade shows, as well as commercials, videos, and promotional films. It was the first time I felt I was truly in charge of the big picture. Choreography and all its minutiae—staging, wardrobe, set design, music—became my passion, and soon I was working as a choreographer and director around the globe. Yet something was missing.

At twenty-five, I returned to Los Angeles from Paris, where I had been choreographing the Lido on the Champs-Élysées. Somehow, the beautiful apartment that I'd been renting didn't

feel right. I knew I wanted something of my own, something more permanent—the sense of home I had never fully felt before. I ended up buying a 1920s Spanish house and living there for twenty years, longer than anywhere else in my life. It was there that Jeff the interior designer was born. I overhauled that home over and over, never feeling that I was wasting money or time—renovating, redecorating, rearranging! I adored seeing the transformation of that space. Over time, I had also become the person my friends would call when they needed to revamp their interiors. After many years of choreographing across the world and soaking up inspiration, I felt I needed a career change, and interior design—the only thing I was equally excited by—was it. My dear friend Eleanor Mondale hired me to renovate her homes and gave me the confidence to pursue design as a new career. Before too long I was designing spaces for other amazingly inventive people, including celebrities like Ryan Seacrest, Khloé Kardashian, Michael C. Hall, Kris Jenner, Kourtney Kardashian, and Kaley Cuoco. I had long been creating glamour for high-profile sports brands, but now I was creating glamour for people that reflected their personalities and the myriad ways they live.

Glamour is achieved not only through extravagance, but also restraint. From the smallest details to the grandest gestures, from the mix of elements to the simplicity of selection. Glamour is a state of mind: living your life in a home that makes you happy, surrounded by things that bring you joy. All hand-picked, collected, and curated in the most original and beautiful ways.

Creating beautiful homes that are well designed, comfortable, and reflective of the personalities of the people who live there is my goal as a designer. Through a generous mix of periods and styles, unexpected lighting, the use of color, texture, and pattern, as well as strong attention to detail, I take it one room at a time, always with my eye on the big picture, to create a home that is finished but with room to evolve with the people living in it. And yes, there is always glamour!

To create a cohesive home that flows smartly from one room
to the next, take a step back and look at the big picture.

Cinematic Style

The rooms that silver-screen sirens once luxuriated in may be gone, but the atmosphere of those spellbinding spaces can be re-created today. I'm not only referring to glitz and high drama. The right bold gestures—graphic patterns and organic shapes that interplay theatrically—can bring radiant life to a room. Everyone deserves a home that is comfortable, personal, and elegant—a home that brings you happiness every time you walk in the door.

Grand Journey

Decorating a home can be a lesson in persistence. By the time the couple who own this Northern California home reached out to me, they had been through several designers—and frankly, they hadn't had the best experiences. They're such a genuine, interesting, and fun pair, and I desperately wanted to show them they could create the home they desired *and* relish the process. When you're designing your home, the journey is every bit as important as the destination—you won't appreciate the final product as much if you don't delight in getting there.

These clients are drawn to neutrals that are subdued and low-key. They wanted their home to have a sophisticated, old-world quality—but with a modern kick, and elements of surprise. The sedate palette running throughout includes countless shades of gray, all of which come together for calming continuity. As a backdrop, gray is fantastic. It complements and contrasts other colors in a harmonious way, but it never begs for attention.

Because the home is very open and grand, I made a concerted effort to design rooms that were more than just beautiful—they're welcoming. The design is as warm as possible; I didn't want it to feel cold and cavernous, like some ersatz castle on a hill. The resulting overall feeling is textural and layered and slightly moody—it has a European flavor with rustic qualities, emphasized by my selection of French limestone floors and antiques sprinkled throughout. So while all the rooms share a palette for tranquil consistency, each one has its own voice, which seems to greet you as you move throughout the home.

OPPOSITE: An age-old stone mantel imparts a decidedly European feel in a Northern California wine-country manse. FOLLOWING PAGES: Antiqued mirrors double the space and add a contemplative air to the living room, where a custom mirror-top cocktail table and sofas by Jeff Andrews for A. Rudin flank the fireplace.

A dream home is filled with exceptional memories. Your best life stories reflect your personal glamour.

When the time came to consider art and finishing touches, my clients revealed they had crates of finds from their travels to Jaipur, India, in storage, including a resplendent white peacock and carved wooden and stone artifacts. It was so amazing to unpack their long-hidden treasures and surround them with memories of their travels! Living with things that have meaning to you is essential to achieving your dream house. Your collections carry so much emotional significance; they're key to making interiors feel "done." Just remember to leave a bit of room for growth and evolution. Life keeps evolving, and so should your home.

We injected glamour into every room in the form of chandeliers. My client loves pretty objects and feminine touches and as we worked together, we kept joking with each other that we were creating a truly pampering escape: "Oh, life really sparkles under chandeliers!" When you finally have the home you've been longing for, it should feel replete with meaning and happy recollections at every turn.

OPPOSITE, CLOCKWISE FROM TOP LEFT: Styling objects symmetrically unites them in a calm manner, whatever their origin. A timeworn stone sculpture echoes photographs by Man Ray in the dining room and serves as an homage to his famous chess-inspired art. The glimmering crystal chandelier balances the expansive dining table. Finds from the homeowners' travels make this a home like no other.

PREVIOUS PAGES: A reclaimed fireplace
mantel supplies a sense of history in the
cozy sunken sitting area. Curated,
collected souvenirs atop the mantel imbue
the space with international appeal.
RIGHT: A Shattered rug from the Jeff
Andrews Collection for Mansour Modern
adds modern edge to the traditional
vibe; silver-leaf wallpaper on the dining
room ceiling reflects flattering light.

OPPOSITE: In the kitchen, vintage French crystal pendants echo the silver-leaf mirror-tiled backsplash timelessly. ABOVE: A rustic table and antique wooden dough bowls evoke a Tuscan farmhouse. FOLLOWING PAGES: Grass-cloth walls with metallic stud details add vertical graphic quality in the media room.

ABOVE: An antique mirror set playfully atop a mirrored tile wall adds a theatrical
moment to the powder room, which is sheathed in Jeff Andrews's Forged
wallpaper for Astek. OPPOSITE: Feminine touches—from the crystal chandeliers to
the lines of a limestone mantel—bestow an amiable demeanor on the home.

Feminine shapes and a dreamy color
palette of powder blues, bronze,
and creams evoke a period boudoir with
a modern sensibility. The gilded bed
finished with platinum leaf is custom and
upholstered in silk; the silk-and-wool rug
is made up of fifteen different colors
and has a painterly quality that supplies
a contemporary note to the space.

I love mixing vintage pieces into every interior. The collision of old and new is magic.

A mirrored bedside table visually doubles beloved collections, such as this vignette of vintage and contemporary pottery. Including a variety of shapes and textures in a ceramic grouping adds contrast.

ABOVE: Delicate patterns keep the focus on the idyllic country view in the vanity of the master bath. OPPOSITE: A deep soaking tub is the consummate perch for watching the light change across the surrounding landscape. A trifecta of pendant lights made from semiprecious stones provide a dose of heady glitz long after the sun goes down.

Elegant/Proportions

Elegant is one of those words that means different things to different people. Within the context of interior design, many think of elegance as buttoned-up formality—rooms that are meant to be seen, but not truly *used*. To me, the opposite is true: an elegant room is aesthetically beautiful and put together, yes, but it also has to be livable—and that's where proportion comes in.

Take this Hidden Hills, California, family home of an NBA star and his chic wife, which perfectly suits my definition of elegance. It was a brand-new spec home when I began designing the interiors, and the directive from the clients was simple: they wanted it to be fabulous, but in a way that felt personal to them. I worked with them closely to breathe a youthful energy and style into each room.

I'm often drawn to monochromatic color schemes, where I determine one hue and build on it. They're anything but boring—they require layers and layers of texture and a gentle progression of one color. The results are soothing and calming; energy comes from the disparate patterns and finishes used. In the entryway, muted metallics create a common thread that runs throughout the home. Because the vaulted ceilings are dramatic and high but the room itself isn't extremely large, a vintage Lucite chandelier draws your eyes up into the space. In oversize paisley, the wallpaper is unexpected, supplying instant character; the antiqued mirrored table catches the light, supplying just a hint of sophisticated flash.

In the living room, I utilized symmetry for calm and familiarity—but kept things lively with surprising touches, such as sculptural agave roots I'd found in Palm Springs. The pair of mirrors tipped toward the room were an homage to those you see in Parisian restaurants; tilting them both expands the space and draws you

OPPOSITE: A vintage Lucite chandelier leads the eye up into the foyer's vaulted ceilings in this California ranch home, while oversize paisley wallpaper keeps it playful. FOLLOWING PAGES: Metallic upholstery and finishes in silvers and golds emanate sophisticated sparkle, connoting that this sitting area is always champagne-ready.

Sheer silk drapery in the living room magnifies design drama, from the rafters to the fabric puddling on the floor.

Monochromatic color schemes are anything but boring. They require layers of texture and gentle progression of one hue for captivating results.

in. The overall effect is overtly glamorous, especially alongside the sheer drapery that hangs from the high beamed ceiling and allows light to flow.

I covered the walls of a hallway adjacent to the master bedroom in a chunky woven grass cloth, adding texture and warming up the space. A piece of driftwood is an organic statue, taking pride of place in an alcove. The custom light fixture I designed with antique Moroccan brass pendants emits a well-traveled aura. Sometimes, it's the in-between spaces that can have the most drama.

I departed a bit from the home's main color scheme in the master bedroom, because it is pivotal to connote the division between public and private. Couples' bedrooms require a perfect balance of masculine and feminine; here, that's evident in the shapely furniture silhouettes paired with dark masculine colors. Much of the furniture in this home is custom to suit the homeowner's height, and the bed was no exception—it's eight feet by eight feet (remember, he's a basketball star). The bed serves as the foundation for the entire space and is an instant focal point, with inviting velvet tufting.

Proportion is a vital part of design cohesiveness. There are no rules for balancing scale—it's about what feels right. Still, I find that sometimes, in smaller rooms, large furniture helps a space seem bigger. When dimensions are wrong, any semblance of elegance vanishes. But when each piece's footprint is correct, everything clicks into place like a puzzle, for a flawless fit.

Zebra-print chairs play against the adjacent living room's rug for a cohesive flow between spaces. Hurricane candles cast a soft, fairy-tale glow over the entire party; an art piece made from lacquered magazine ads furnishes a necessary injection of creative energy.

Proportion is such a vital part of design cohesiveness. There are no rules for balancing scale—it's about what feels right. The interplay of varying shapes and sizes adds rich dimension.

OPPOSITE: A hand-carved wooden mirror and elegant brass opera chairs take pride of place in the bedroom foyer. The light fixture is an assemblage of antique Moroccan brass pendants retrofitted for electricity. FOLLOWING PAGES: Chunky woven wallcoverings add texture and make a space feel finished—with less need for art and embellishment—and also bestow enveloping warmth.

The homeowners' Louis Vuitton trunk made an ideal cocktail table in their office, which is lined in masculine wood paneling. Velvet ikat-upholstered antique chairs inject a burst of dramatic color.

Timeless/Illumination

Some houses are an architectural test of courage. When my clients, a family with three young kids, purchased this Hollywood Hills home, it nearly doubled their living space, but it had significant problems with its layout—the flow just wasn't conducive to their lifestyle. We took everything down to the studs and reimagined the architecture to suit their specific needs, adding larger windows to make it feel more open and contemporary, relocating the kitchen to the literal center of the home, and even redesigning the grand staircase to be even more grand (and yet child-friendly). The family loved a few of my previous projects and gave me carte blanche on my vision; they simply asked that their home have a European, personalized flavor.

Light fixtures play an integral role in each space. In the entry hall, smoky quartz crystals captivate from the suspended custom fixture. I didn't want a typical chandelier in this foyer—it had to be something I'd never seen before, something sculptural and creative, and it needed to be large-scale to hold its own within its grand locale. The crystals on this piece catch daylight so they appear to glow from within; the trifecta of circles, like ripples on a still pond, draw your eye up to the sky-high ceiling. In the dining room, the sole purpose is spending time with family, so I selected a focal point with je ne sais quoi in the form of light fixtures from 1910. They impart a regal, old-world, extravagant tone that fits with the antique limestone flooring, and their generous size echoes the expansive table. The gold art piece hung above the mantel lends a necessary modern edge, counterbalancing the overtly traditional and preventing it from appearing contrived.

An ethereal, iridescent crystal light fixture suits the generous scale in the master bedroom and sets a peaceful tone. The entire master suite is restful, with its sleek gray walls and soothing color palette. Four-poster beds are

OPPOSITE: A custom smoky-quartz chandelier captivates in the marble-and-limestone-floored entry, where horizontally textured wallpaper accentuates the curved walls. Modern art placed throughout this Hollywood Hills home keeps its grand, European look fresh. FOLLOWING PAGES: A gold wall sculpture by artist Aldo Chaparro provides a distinct counterbalance to the dining room's old-world ambience, with an antique limestone mantel and floors as well as light fixtures from a 1910 bank.

Contemporary touches complement the youthful energy of the homeowners—overly traditional pieces would have looked contrived in this particular architectural style. Textured wood tiles from Jeff Andrews for Jamie Beckwith Collection on the built-in bookcase highlight the curated collections.

56

ABOVE: Combining throw pillows in both graphic and organic patterns in natural fabrics creates a light, celebratory mood in the bar's lounge area. OPPOSITE: Chandeliers made of LED-illuminated rock-crystal rings are an exercise in symmetry and maximizing space.

Layering different periods and styles will elevate your experience of a space.

fantastic for defining large spaces like this, because they're stately and commanding—especially when they have contemporary lines. The look is evocative of a luxury hotel, yet it feels like home. Separate his-and-hers bathrooms and closets at either end of the master bedroom were a welcome opportunity to design at the epitome of both masculine and feminine, never feeling like I had to walk the tightrope between them. His bath was all dark stone and hard lines; hers was a lesson in ladylike white on white: I mixed varying shades and textures to create dimension with the mirror, mother-of-pearl inlay, and gilded wallpaper.

I took a similar tack in the kitchen, which is my take on the quintessential white kitchen so many homeowners long for. It's classic and sophisticated, yet there's no actual white in here. Everything is a shade of gray or cream, accented by antique gold fixtures, hardware, French oak floors, and quartzite counters. The marriage of both age-old and modern lines means it will age timelessly.

Each room in this home is a tribute to the transformative power of light. Illumination is as essential as air, and yet there's a polar difference between a fresh breeze and a stifling one—chandeliers, sconces, and lamps are the same way. I selected each light source with one truism in mind: let there be light, and let it be bewitching.

OPPOSITE, CLOCKWISE FROM TOP LEFT: Hand-hewn pottery imbues any space with a creative pulse. An awkward, unused closet is transformed into a temperature-controlled wine cellar that puts bottles on artful display against an antique firebrick wall; the custom arched factory window took its cues from the bottoms of wine bottles. Art pieces made of repurposed wooden skateboards impart California cool. The indoor/outdoor bar is sheathed in wood tiles from Jeff Andrews for Jamie Beckwith Collection. FOLLOWING PAGES: A crisp take on the all-white kitchen isn't white at all, but rather shades of cream and gray accented with antiqued gold hardware. Light fixtures are the opposite of industrial, with gem-inspired silhouettes that adorn the kitchen like fine jewelry.

Dramatic lighting is key to supplying spaces with theatrical moments. A sculptural fixture can help write the script for the rest of the room.

OPPOSITE, CLOCKWISE FROM TOP LEFT: Collecting objects in a similar color palette helps them retain a tranquil, uncluttered appearance. Textured walls help create a restful quality in a generously sized master bedroom. An ethereal, shimmering glass chandelier above a round table gives you a visual kick as you enter the room and separates the bed from the sitting area. Sculptural furniture from the Jeff Andrews for A. Rudin collection with natural linen upholstery says relax.

PREVIOUS PAGES: When you're blessed with the luxury of space in a master bedroom, divide the sleeping area from the sitting room with a moment of beauty to kick up the glamour factor. The four-poster bed reinforces the lines of the coffered ceiling and is paired with symmetrically placed furniture and objets.
RIGHT: The master bedroom's sitting area is an exercise in symmetry, even texturally: the antique mirrors have a symbiotic relationship with the antiqued-mirror cocktail tables. Design choices—from the tête-à-tête to the travertine fireplace surround—work together in a sophisticated, tranquil way that suits a bedroom.

PREVIOUS PAGES, LEFT: Setting unexpected sculptures before a mirror—such as this modern bust sculpture by Corey Ellis in the master bedroom—doubles their impact. PREVIOUS PAGES, RIGHT: In the "his" master bathroom, veined marble countertops echo the slab-marble shower along with the parquet checkerboard hand-cut marble floor tiles. Faceted pendants catch the light, day or night.

RIGHT: Pink-and-white ink-on-paper pieces by Bettina Mauel provide a jolt of energetic color in the white-on-white "hers" master bathroom, where varying hues lend the space necessary dimension, and inlaid mother-of-pearl tile in the flooring resembles an area rug.

Star
Quality

Star quality is intangible—but when you have the It factor, it resonates on all levels. The same is true for interiors. When you've put together a scene so note-perfect, you can't imagine it any other way, you've cast a mesmerizing, unforgettable spell that can be felt throughout your entire home. Each and every room should be sprinkled with a good dose of indelible design magic.

Theatrical/Sophistication

When I first met Kris Jenner, I was already working with her daughter Khloé, and I had designed a home for Ryan Seacrest that she *loved*. Kris had definite ideas on how to renovate this house—a Mediterranean-inspired manse—and a vision for transforming it into her dream home. We started working together by redesigning a single guest room. Once our relationship opened up and the trust factor was there, we embarked on redesigning the entire interior together.

We kept to a strict schedule, segregating parts of the home that would be usable for both living and filming her reality show during the renovation. Kris is a real no-nonsense person, and time was of the essence, so it became a bit like orchestrating a production. I selected all the elements making sure to use either ready-made materials or hiring artisans who could deliver on-deadline, while maintaining the design at top caliber.

Kris's directive for her home was old-Hollywood glamour, but in a way that made sense with her lifestyle and family. It needed to be functional *and* stunning. Kris's sophistication level is undeniable—she has soaked up so much about taste and style throughout her amazing life—so when we embarked on this renovation, she had a checklist of influences and inspirations. We formed a true collaboration: I would present things to her, and she would say things like, "I love that, I love that, kick this up a notch, make this more dramatic, tone this down a little." It was all about finding a balance.

Kris Jenner's original dining chairs were reupholstered in a burgundy-and-muted gold fabric reminiscent of corsetry, which lends feminine strength to the otherwise traditional seating.
FOLLOWING PAGES: A gold dress mannequin stands watch over the grand entry, an ode to old Hollywood in the form of black-and-white checkered-marble floors, a sweeping redesigned staircase, and an antique light fixture salvaged from a 1920s movie theater.

The checkered black-and-white marble floors on the first floor were Kris's idea, and the second she said it, I thought, Perfect! *Done!* They set a graphic tone for the whole house. Because it's such a strong statement, other areas are more subdued, devoid of bright patterns or any competing colors. I upgraded the staircase's painted wooden spindles with a custom iron-forged baluster that suited the overall design and installed a 1920s fixture that had hung in a lavish theater in its previous life.

When I think of old-Hollywood glamour, my mind is instantly transported to the Art Deco era. Throughout the home, hints of Deco call that period to mind—without being too obvious—such as the antique sconces, Kyle Bunting hide rug in a chevron pattern, and shapely furniture in the formal living room. It's a modern homage that comes together to create a quiet, sophisticated, and peaceful space. The master bathroom doubles as a "glam room" where the magic happens for Kris and the girls, and it needed to suit the rest of the home. The marble floor pattern is reminiscent of Coco Chanel, with its black and white chain-link pattern, and the fixtures in her closet are vintage Lalique pendants Kris had found. The glamour never ends!

Kris's master bedroom was the last phase of our renovation, and with the rest of the home firmly established, I knew I could take the design to a different level. The wildly graphic area rug grounds the room, letting the rest of the interior stay luxe and tranquil. The bed is custom channeled-silk velvet; the lamps are antique carved gilt, preserved forever in Lucite; and the Jean de Merry bedside tables are fitted with Lucite-and-bronze drawer handles—an exceedingly Deco moment. Behind the bifold mirrors, I installed a custom coffee bar for convenience.

There are many beautiful pieces in this home that hold personal meaning for Kris, including three crystal chandeliers from previous residences. I convinced her to hang them at different levels in one room—the dining room—so they would have a stronger effect. Touches like that combined to create a perfect backdrop for the life that goes on within the home—it didn't feel like designing a set, yet it ended up looking incredibly cinematic on TV.

OPPOSITE: Antique Art Deco sconces illuminate a freestanding custom mirror in Kris's sitting room, where shapely furniture softens the antique French limestone fireplace surround. FOLLOWING PAGES: Windows in the sitting room were replaced with rounded doors to open up the space and allow natural light to flow.

There's just as much theater in the details of a room as the grand gestures. Strong design choices on every level, big and small, create the glamorous edge.

Bronze metallic grass cloth by Maya Romanoff and a silver-leaf ceiling reflect twinkling light from Kris's trio of chandeliers, each from her former homes.

OPPOSITE: Inspired by French country kitchens, but with Los Angeles verve, Kris's kitchen is a clean slate—an ideal backdrop for the colorful personalities that enliven the home. ABOVE: Vintage Murano white glass chandeliers add a note of glitz above the pair of oversize islands.

A silk shag rug and plush lounge
furniture give the family room a
particularly inviting feel. Because of the
room's unconventional shape, it's
divided into separate entertaining areas,
including a bar and TV lounge.

Metals and metallic finishes as well as colors derived from them can play a striking role in design. The depth of field from silvers, golds, bronze, and copper add contrast and richness to any color scheme

The family room's dark color palette—with metallic wood-veneer wallpaper in a chevron pattern—is a warm, enveloping departure from the rest of the home. Feminine art pieces with sanguine spirit delight the eye.

PREVIOUS PAGES: A graphic area rug grounds the master bedroom, where luxurious touches take center stage, including a channeled-silk velvet bed and Deco-inspired Lucite-and-bronze bedside tables. The bifold mirrored closet doors open to reveal a coffee bar. ABOVE: Antiqued mirror-inlaid surfaces add the illusion of more space in an already spacious closet. Wallpapering the ceiling in an Hermès pattern brings it down to earth—glamorously. OPPOSITE: In the master bathroom, floor tiles that pay homage to Chanel continue the classic tone.

Captivating / Spirit

The first day I met actress Kaley Cuoco, she said, "I'm going to be your easiest client, because I love your taste and I love what you do!" That was no lie. She's the quickest decision maker. Kaley asked for a home with vibrant energy—something that captured her own voice. Her personality is positive, genuine, and happy, so I made a place that reflects that, using a profusion of color and elements of surprise.

Kaley purchased the home from another client of mine—Khloé Kardashian—and little by little we tweaked here and made adjustments there, until we had renovated most of the home to suit her own style. Kaley radiates a love of life, so as our relationship grew, I kept my eye out for pieces that were truly "her."

Take the living room—exuberance incarnate! Kaley had asked for it to be really bright, light, happy, and colorful. A painting inspired the color palette and even the feeling, which is young and fresh yet decidedly retro. Kaley is so drop-dead funny that it felt as if I was translating her cheerful disposition into the design itself. Note the swing—who doesn't want a swing in their house? The custom rug contains hues from the painting, and the furniture—in unexpected shapes—creates a mood that says, "Come in, have a drink, and stay a while." The walls and ceiling are sheathed with a wallcovering from my own collection; it was inspired by vintage ceramic glazes,

OPPOSITE: The circular entry hall in Kaley Cuoco's Los Angeles home calls for an inventive round table, such as this sculptural brass piece that evokes a tree trunk.
FOLLOWING PAGES: The metallic Carved wallcovering in White Gold by Jeff Andrews for Astek reflects the dazzling LED light of a multitude of custom crystal pendants.

96

and its slightly metallic white gold finish is a perfect foil for the room's cacophony of colors. The cut crystal-and-brass pendants are reminiscent of raindrops.

Because Kaley has a great love of animals and is an accomplished equestrian, I used fauna throughout the home, in sculpture, wallpaper, and beyond. In the entryway, the sculptural brass table flows with the round shape of the room and plays well with the brass horse sculptures along the wall. In the dining room, Kaley owned a stunning painting that we pulled inspiration from, such as the vintage malachite pieces on the sideboard and vintage chairs reupholstered in emerald fabric and faux-fur seats. It all makes for a cohesive color story that's easy on the eyes. When I first discovered the Hermès horse wallpaper now living in the kitchen's breakfast nook, I texted it to Kaley. Her response: "Um, *yes!*" It's black and white, with little touches of chartreuse and accents of Hermès orange—it's like visual candy, and it's so her. You can't go wrong with black, white, and a strong color.

For Kaley's kitchen, her directive again was "bright and happy." The timeless gray color palette complements the limestone floors running throughout. But of course, I didn't want it to be boring or stale in any way, so I put a graphic patterned wallpaper, again from my collection, on the ceiling and installed hand-cut marble mosaic tiles on the walls. Gray is a neutral, but it has so much more depth than most whites; I often pick a warm gray if I'm blending with warmer colors or metallics, like the antiqued brass accents here.

Like life itself, design is always a work in progress. Your home is a state of being as well as a physical place—we need to pay attention to the way things make us *feel* as well as the way things look—and getting it right doesn't happen overnight.

OPPOSITE, CLOCKWISE FROM TOP LEFT: In the sunken living room, the sofa's feminine, curvaceous lines foil the room's hard edges. An artisan-made cocktail table hewn of bronze and recycled glass bottles is its own form of art, especially placed above a Kyle Bunting rug with colors pulled from a nearby painting. A sculptural credenza forms a sexy base for a vintage art piece Kaley calls "Das Boot." Hot pink velvet chairs are a welcoming perch with excellent proximity to the bar.

ABOVE: A variety of fabrics and finishes combine to give the living room a throwback-to-the-'70s feel in a refreshing, energetic palette. The fireplace surround is Arabascato marble. OPPOSITE: A bronze-and-leather sling-seat swing by BDDW is a functional art piece that also furnishes the space with fun.

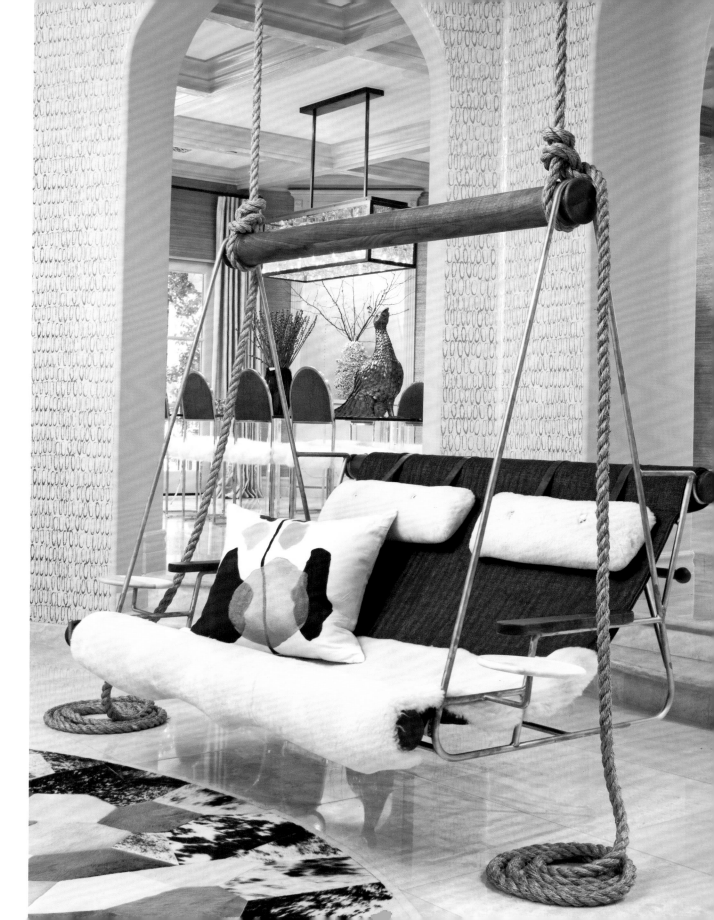

In a colorful home be selective about where you use graphic patterns and where you opt for calm, cool textures. This allows them to catch the eye but not overwhelm.

OPPOSITE: Imbued with a touch of Zsa Zsa Gabor, the dining room's streamlined glass-and-Lucite table is flanked by both klismos and brass-and-faux fur chairs for retro, unflappably cool glamour. FOLLOWING PAGES, LEFT: Vintage malachite and art pieces continue the color narrative. FOLLOWING PAGES, RIGHT: When it's illuminated, a light fixture made of one-way mirrors reveals what appear to be wine goblets within. A graphic painting from Kaley's collection formed the color catalyst for the rest of the space.

Mixing materials in an unexpected way, such as wallpaper on the ceiling, adds an element of design surprise. Each room deserves a sense of fun! Personality is paramount.

Mixing patterns and finishes—such as the hand-cut marble mosaic walls, antiqued brass, and stainless steel in Kaley's kitchen—is key to making a space original. The wallpaper on the ceiling is Jeff Andrews for Astek, and it creates a strong dichotomy with the geometric walls.

ABOVE: A dark antiqued-brass salamander sconce adds a note of the unexpected to the kitchen wall. OPPOSITE: Gray is a neutral—the new beige. Added details, such as hammered darkened-copper sinks, a custom mug rack, and artfully displayed objets on open shelving, keep it interesting.

OPPOSITE: Hermès wallpaper depicting racing horses is a chic homage to Kaley's equestrian side. ABOVE: Take the proverbial pop of color into a contemporary setting subtly—as with the vibrant orange and lime-green accents in the breakfast nook—and it won't be cliché.

Whimsical / Balancing Act

When Kourtney Kardashian enlisted me to design her home, she told me to disregard typical design rules. "I want my house to be really whimsical, like *Alice in Wonderland*," she said. Kourtney was the third member of the Kardashian family I had the opportunity to work with, and she has an innate design sensibility. She adores vintage and modern things that have a distinctive edge, so collaborating with her on this home was a real pleasure—we saw eye to eye.

Upon moving in, Kourtney painted the entire interior with a fresh coat of bright white paint, making it a completely blank canvas. We began injecting energy and a sense of history throughout the home with color and pattern, starting with the living room. Kourtney knew she wanted black and white stripes from the beginning—a bold statement, certainly, but Kourtney's not one to shy away from anything like that. I decided lining the walls in large horizontal stripes would give the effect she'd asked for without overdoing it, and I softened the look with numerous simple glass-globe pendants that are reminiscent of Alice's trip to Wonderland. We pulled the hues in the room from pieces Kourtney already owned, such as the peacock-feather headdress on the black-lacquered mantel. This room has drama, but the carefully considered mix of elements prevent it from going over the top— there's a fine line between whimsical design and a circus, and a black and white scheme with minimal injections of a bright color are easy on the eye and extremely livable.

To create a seamless transition with the living room, I used smaller, more delicate stripes in the adjoining playroom on the ceiling and walls. Since this area is designed for Kourtney's kids, nothing is too precious or fragile—the room's only purpose is to be fun, starting with the splashy light fixture. Her father's piano anchors the space; from there, we brought in a few hot-pink touches, carefully collected.

OPPOSITE: Black-and-white Hermès wallpaper in the foyer allows Crayola-bright art to pop. FOLLOWING PAGES: Kourtney Kardashian requested an *Alice in Wonderland* interior, like the horizontal black and white stripes in the not-so-formal living room. Clear globe pendant lamps and earthy turquoise elements keep it sophisticated.

Bold pieces and graphic patterns have to be used confidently yet subtly to stand the test of time.

I wanted the family room to feel separate from the rest of the house and have its own slightly more eclectic aura. The hand-painted wallpaper resembles the endpapers of an antique book, which imbues the space with an artisanal quality. The generous mix of patterned fabrics is still whimsical, albeit in a more muted color scheme; the collection of antique horns on the mantel and a vintage Moroccan rug give the room a well-traveled sensibility.

In Kourtney's bedroom, the neon sign she chose to hang above the bed is flanked by two vintage lamps that were a gift from her mom. The textural wallpaper looks similar to malachite, and the chevron silk curtains and dappled carpet give the space complexity—in softer hues to prevent it from becoming gaudy. I custom designed the plush channeled headboard and the TV cabinet at the foot of the bed, which is wrapped in soft shagreen.

Kourtney loves vintage finds—which is evident the moment you enter the house. The palatial foyer contains antique pieces she collected herself over the years. The Hermès wallpaper highlights the sky-high ceiling by drawing the eye upward. The childlike spheres on the floor, made of wood and concrete, tell you immediately that this home has a sense of humor!

The key to creating a whimsical home is imbuing it with playful Seussian pieces, but tempering them with enough dignified colors and finishes that they're not overwhelming. It's similar to arranging a vase of flowers: there's a reason florists often use simple stems of greens to offset bursts of firework-like peonies. They help focus attention on what really matters. Balance makes beauty.

OPPOSITE: Symmetrical styling can create tranquility even in rooms where bold, unconventional statements—such as the regal Dobermans, chinoiserie bench, and vintage sconces—are the norm. FOLLOWING PAGES: In a playroom created for Kourtney's children, things aren't always so black and white: nothing in the space is too precious for kids to handle, including the horn chair and even her father's piano.

ABOVE: The white-on-white styling of Kourtney's outdoor seating area makes it a crisp and calming hideaway. OPPOSITE: Kourtney's hand-me-down chairs add the sweetness of memory to her eat-in kitchen, where graphic chevron window treatments nod to the stripes in the adjacent family room. The custom table was made of vintage brass ram heads and a black glass top.

PREVIOUS PAGES: Hand-painted wallpaper
reminiscent of antique book endpapers
cozies up the family room, a compara-
tively sedate departure from the rest of
the home. The vintage Moroccan rug
from Mansour Modern pulls all elements
of the room—the antique horns on the
mantel, the patterned throw pillows on the
enveloping sectional—together cohesively.
RIGHT: Silk window treatments and
malachite-inspired wallcoverings create
textural complexity in Kourtney's master
bedroom. The shagreen-sheathed custom
cabinet at the foot of the bed hides a
television; the vintage bedside lamps were
a gift from Kourtney's mom Kris.

Livable Glamour

In order to last, beauty must be livable, and that counts doubly so in your home. You spend the vast majority of your life there, which necessitates both opulence and ease. It can be both, I promise. For perpetual glamour, your decorating should appeal to all the senses: scent, sound, touch, and, of course, sight. That's a recipe for enchantment each time you walk through your door.

Chic/Escape

Designing a getaway home is a bit like picking out your vacation wardrobe—you want it to look markedly different from your everyday experience of living, so you can truly *relax*. This newly built Manhattan Beach family retreat belongs to a beloved longtime client of mine—I call her Lady—who asked for it to have a look of understated luxury. I had designed three previous homes for her, and the first time she was just twenty-five years old. She is now a wife and mother, so this home had significantly different needs: it required exceptional design, of course, but it also needed a level of laissez-faire (that is, it had to withstand playful growing children and a revolving door of guests).

Because this isn't her full-time home, she wanted it to be a bit less layered, which lends itself to the unfettered vacation vibe. The house sits directly on the sand, which led to a comfortable California-coastal mood. I call it laid-back chic: it gives you a soothing, tranquil feeling whenever you're there.

In any beachfront home, the view is really the art—the star of the show. Almost everything about this design is meant to lead your eye to the seascape beyond the windows in a warm and inviting way, so I didn't clutter it up with unnecessary furniture. In the master bedroom, I designed a cozy built-in captain's bed that faces the water, with antiqued mirror behind the headboard to reflect the beach and add another dimension. It still has all the functionality of a traditional bed—with a soft headboard, reading lamps, and shelves that are illuminated at night—but it's evocative of its place. In the adjacent seating area, an enveloping sectional and sturdy teak tables inspired by garden furniture create a retreat within a retreat. There is a slightly nautical spirit here and throughout the home, from the beadboard walls leading into the bedroom to the round porthole window in the master bath.

OPPOSITE: Driftwood and sand inspired the palette of the seafront dining room, where a space-saving built-in banquette provides additional storage for cushions and children's toys. FOLLOWING PAGES: Natural finishes like weathered teak and sun-bleached fabric choices combine to epitomize laid-back chic.

There's boundless beauty in nature.

A color palette can be inspired by what's around you—like the sea glass, seashell, sand, and driftwood hues here.

Historic-looking touches, such as beadboard ceilings, rattan counter stools, and 1920s light fixtures evoke a nautical feel in the kitchen.

Guest bedrooms themselves are destinations, a vacation within the comforts of home. Because they're often tucked away behind closed doors, they can be a refreshing departure from the rest of the house. So here, I designed an original brass chandelier out of vintage globes and balanced it with playful hand-blocked linen that formed the color scheme. My approach with children's rooms is to let the kids be involved in the design of their world, without allowing it to become overly juvenile. Here, that meant subtle nods to the beach beyond (ship's-wheel sconces, a sparkling seahorse pendant lamp) with pieces that would make them feel at home, such as a fluffy shag rug and upholstery prints in their favorite colors.

The color palette of this home rose from the ocean itself. Pieces of sea glass, a seashell, sand, and driftwood formed a starting point, and hues inspired by them flowed from room to room. In the kitchen, the tongue-and-groove ceiling is glazed a pale blue that contrasts with the creamy white support beams, which add depth; reclaimed wood on the island exudes a driftwood feel. The backsplash, in handmade and hand-glazed terra-cotta, gives homespun texture to the space. Light fixtures from the 1920s were remade for today; they make the room more personal, intimate, and inviting, and unlike recessed lighting, they are extremely flattering! In the adjacent open living room and eating nook, 1970s carved-wood chairs with caned seats and a risk-taking, large-print upholstery fabric set a playful tone. The built-in banquette at the farmhouse table ensures everyone can face the view, with the added bonus of extra storage beneath the seats for towels and toys. Since small rooms are an opportunity to do something more dramatic, the powder room's walls are lined in silver-leafed terra-cotta tile in arabesque shapes—another chance to make a tiny space sing. The faucet is unlacquered brass, which is perfect for the beach; the finish oxidizes more quickly in the salty air, giving it a natural patina that says seaside at a glance.

No one wants to enter his or her vacation home and be reminded of real-life stresses and strains, so it is important that the decor is a palpable departure from the norm. Every hue and surface in the common areas combine to cast a calming, spa-like spell that's a long way from ordinary. It's all part of creating a separate world—one you adore so much, you can't wait to return to it.

Even a powder room can exude carefree glamour. This one imitates its Manhattan Beach locale with arabesque-shaped wall tiles in a subtle silver-leaf finish, reminiscent of shells.

Hues that flow from room to room are key to making an entire home cohesive.

A chic escape is created by balancing color, texture, and comfort.

In-between spaces, like hallways, set the tone for what's to come. This passageway, lined in beadboard, has picture ledges for the homeowner's collection of miniature landscape and abstract paintings. Personalization is everything.

RIGHT: A custom built-in bed took its cues from those of nineteenth-century sea captains and includes an antiqued mirror that reflects the sea view, so you can watch the waves roll in from any angle. FOLLOWING PAGES, LEFT: Seafoam green subway tiles wrap a master bathroom, supplying a sense of history. FOLLOWING PAGES, RIGHT: A homespun turned-wood chandelier calls to mind a ship's steering wheel in the master bedroom's sitting area. Slatted teak tables are meant to evoke laid-back garden furniture.

ABOVE: The secret to decorating children's rooms: mixing textural patterns that are bold, intricate, and striped—in one color they love—for playful tension between the prints. OPPOSITE: In the guest room, the hand-blocked linen on the headboard and shades became the base for the color palette.

Vintage/Edge

I previously designed a beach house for this then-bachelor client of mine, and it was very organic, understated, and neutral. Here, I took a different approach, combining two top-floor units into one sweeping penthouse. He asked for practicality above all else; in addition, he didn't want anything to be drab—he favored rooms with energy and vibrancy.

Once we combined the two original units, the home was essentially a loft-like concrete box—and, frankly, a bit lifeless. I installed antique French oak floorboards to warm it up, and strategically placed area rugs and furniture to create individual living areas within the open floor plan—vital for comfort and flow. The rooms are separated with sliding doors made of opaque colored glass, which preserves the open architecture while allowing the option of closing areas off for privacy. To keep a spirited, unexpected vibe, I placed a slightly retro thread throughout with vintage and custom furniture pieces. The hues of these throwback pieces are deep and saturated, like a Kodachrome film still sprung to life.

Architectural challenges happen often in historic spaces such as this one, but they can lead to unforeseen design opportunities. Since the ceilings here are solid concrete, I hid necessary electrical wiring in creative ways, such as the modern box-beam ceiling. That allowed for utilitarian necessities under the guise of an architectural statement. In the media room, walls upholstered in suede prevent maddening noise pollution. Not only is the resulting sound amazing,

Vintage pieces, such as these swivel chairs reupholstered in lime green leather, furnish a throwback vibe in a Hollywood penthouse renovation.

Embrace history. Architectural challenges can lead to design opportunities you could never have imagined.

but it also creates an instantaneous feeling of warmth and gives the room its own voice, separate from the rest of the loft.

In keeping with his bachelor status, I utilized masculine pieces such as clean-lined furniture in natural hues and kept any patterns minimal. In one sitting area, a reclaimed slice of a tree trunk serves as sculpture—anything can be art, depending on how it's installed. Art doesn't have to be rare and precious and expensive—even a rustic find such as this one can be a focal point and add spirit to a corner of a home.

Because I wasn't able to tweak the floor plan in the master bathroom, I made it feel special by covering the entire room in tiny glass mosaic tiles, installing niches for towels and toiletries where I could. As a result, it has a Zen-like spa quality that's inherently relaxing—a beautiful effect that may not have happened had I been able to revamp the layout. It's a design lesson for the ages: sometimes, working with what you have precipitates the most creative reinvention.

OPPOSITE: Mirrored doors visually expand the space in the entrance hall, where displayed artifacts combine with a palette of black, white, and burnt orange hues for worldliness. FOLLOWING PAGES: In an apartment, every square inch has to be utilized to its fullest potential. Rugs create separate "rooms" in a loftlike open space with repurposed French-oak flooring. A terrace balcony runs the length of the home and faces west for dreamy sunset views.

Opened-up box beams add the illusion of height to low ceilings in the kitchen and lend more visual interest to the architecture. With hand-glazed, graphic tile, the backsplash has an element of colorful surprise.

The homeowner requested office chairs as dining chairs for their function and comfort; the wool shag rug softens the look. Framed sliding-glass doors between spaces allow light to flow but still provide some privacy.

ABOVE: A custom wool-and-silk Tai Ping rug grounds the master bedroom with graphic style and sparked the design scheme from the bottom up. The linen-upholstered wall adds a layer of hushed softness.
OPPOSITE: Sheathing the small bathroom in tiny glass mosaic tiles imbued it with a soothing, spa-like quality.

Graphic/Living

Continuity is extremely important—there should be a definitive style flow from room to room. I had the opportunity to design this home from the beginning, which allowed me to keep the design as cohesive as possible.

This is a family home with young children, and it had to be relaxing and easygoing as well as chic. These rooms aren't excessively large, so my design directive was to keep them from feeling congested and add dramatic elements with glamorous dimension. The secret? Focus on the lighting—that's the key to supplying intimate spaces with theatrical moments. Each fixture casts a distinct personality on its setting and issues a well-appointed feeling in spaces with an abundance of furniture. The living room's multiple pendants accentuate the double-height ceiling but also draw your eye down into the space; the vintage-inspired lights within the coffered ceiling in the sitting room bestow a storied tenor to this newly built house.

The family entertains frequently, and they requested a formal dining room for dinner parties. The open arches act as a frame for the room, so I decided to treat the entire space as a still life. The Italian Murano-glass fixtures that resemble fluttering handkerchiefs supply an elegant softness; the wallpaper's white-gold metallic accents reflect the light as it changes throughout the day.

When I can, I like to create kitchens that are *more* than kitchens—life revolves around them, so they should have a unique sense of style. Here, I opened it up to create a modernized

Architectural details—rounded doorways, apropos sconces—add historic charm to a newly built house.

158

Every room should have a moment of visual levity: an element of surprise that expresses your personality.

version of the multipurpose great room once found in the great halls and chambers of medieval European castles and estates, with an adjacent living area—but, as this is located in sun-swathed California, there is an outdoor dining room as well. Plenty of people say kitchens are the heart of the home, but for this family, this entire indoor/outdoor great room is truly where they live, and often where they host guests. My clients had asked me for a flow that was seamless throughout, and utilizing a similar palette of buffs and browns, along with muted patterns and textures, I fused each disparate area of the great room into one. The same countertop material—quartzite—is both indoors on the island and outside, to unify the space. There is also artwork, however small, throughout. That's probably the easiest way to turn utilitarian spaces into beautiful rooms: dress them up! Handpicked art can be the final touch that makes a home feel like it is yours.

OPPOSITE: Multiple pendants both accentuate the living room's double-height ceilings and draw the eye down into the cozy space. In a square room, a round rug makes your furniture arrangement more organic and artful. FOLLOWING PAGES: Because the dining room sits largely open—through three arched doorways—to the adjacent hallway, it was treated like a work of art in itself, with handblown Murano-glass chandeliers and metallic wallpaper from Jeff Andrews for Astek.

ABOVE: A coffered ceiling and antiquity-inspired lighting imbue the great room, which adjoins the open kitchen, with timelessness. OPPOSITE: Quartzite countertops have the look and feel of marble without the fragility. The kitchen island contains a multitude of functional elements, including a long plug strip running underneath as a charging station that everyone in the family can use in unison. FOLLOWING PAGES: The great room opens out to an alfresco dining area and the pool. The tabletop is hewn of the counter's same exact quartzite for a cohesive appearance.

Shapes, textures, patterns, and color should be balanced to create harmony. Design is more than visual—it's an experience on a physical level between people and their home.

The bedrooms upstairs are a quiet departure from the more visually energetic ground floor, like this sitting area—an exercise in tailored neutrals.

ABOVE: Because the master bedroom is on the traditional side, the master bathroom is a modern departure—clean and elegant. OPPOSITE: Marble with a linear, almost hand-painted form supplies a graphic element to the room.

Comfort has as much to do with the way we feel as the way things look to the eye. Supply each space with warm details so guests always feel welcome, inside and out.

The outdoor dining area has all the makings for a successful alfresco fete, including a full kitchen replete with a pizza oven. Exquisite custom light fixtures by Paul Ferrante and curtains made of outdoor fabric help ensure an easy indoor/outdoor flow.

The Big Picture

Cinematographers rarely win praise for their close-cropped scenes alone. They take home Academy Awards for their expert combinations of close-ups and panoramas—it's the mix that truly transfixes us. That level of continuity is just as key in design and requisite for making any house a home. When you look around a room, it should be captivating from every view, including curated compositions that reflect your life and style. It's the combination of near and far, detail alongside bold forms, that tells your story and makes your interiors complete.

Detail-Oriented Composition

I've learned that the secret to happy family living is creating a house that's tailor-made to have both welcoming communal spaces and plenty of private retreats for each person to call their own. For this newly built house in L.A.'s Pacific Palisades neighborhood, my clients asked for a chic yet comfortable interior that had a well-collected sensibility and rooms injected with individual personality that also suited their lifestyle. To me, design is not only visual, but also an experience on a physical level through the interaction of people and their environment.

My initial color schemes often start in the heart of the home, such as a formal entry or great room, to set the tone for what's to come. Hues are based on the architecture and the availability of natural light, as well as the existing hard surfaces of the home, such as floors or metalwork, to create a cohesive palette. Once I have the palette for the initial room, I design each room to enhance the overall look. Connectivity is really important, but it has to be subtle! You run the risk of things being contrived if each room doesn't have its own voice. Although homes from the last decade tend to have an open feeling to them, I find people are craving rooms for distinct purposes, so I always design with that in mind.

The entryway can become a destination—not just a pass-through zone. Here, a sculptural and unexpected light fixture mixes with classic, traditional, and interesting vintage furniture pieces to create a look that's timeless and curated with no specific period. I'm constantly combining different styles and materials to find the blend that will elevate the experience of a space.

In the adjacent dining room, the walls are warmed by an oversize paisley-print wallpaper, which adds drama and visual interest to an otherwise very simple room. In a square space, the circular table provides a sense of the infinite, and means there's no bad seat—everyone is at the head of the table. The chairs have a graphic

A collection of vintage pots adds hand-hewn whimsy atop the mantel.

RIGHT: An entryway becomes a veritable destination with the addition of a stream-lined seating area. Vintage finds combine with unorthodox contemporary pieces for a collected appearance. FOLLOWING PAGES: Even in a home with an open feel, it's important to create rooms of distinction. This living-room-turned-music-room stands apart from the rest of the house, thanks to its moody color palette.

quality, especially because I had them ebonized. Every room needs some element of dark for contrast, and to give it depth and detail. This can be achieved through a small gesture, such as curtain hardware or the framing of artwork. It all adds to the overall design complexity. The quiet white-porcelain chandelier put a contemporary take on what could have been a staid, classic element. Spectacular lighting is pivotal to the success of a room.

Because I strive to balance masculine and feminine energy in a home, there is a slightly moodier color scheme in the formal living room to separate it from the rest of the house. The rich, warm tones give this room its own personality. The existing marble fireplace is the room's main focal point, made slightly whimsical with the addition of vintage pots covering the mantel. I'm obsessed with pottery—I buy it everywhere. It has a human, handmade touch that helps put you instantly at ease. The custom oversize mirror along one wall does more than make the room seem larger—it changes the architecture of the space and imparts a different perspective.

A bedroom should reflect who you are and how you spend your time. The massive vintage ceramic lamps inspired this bedroom's design; like the couple that lives here, they're sexy, sophisticated, and commanding. Because this particular space has a high vaulted ceiling, the hand-painted wallpaper and embroidered silk window treatments ground the room, adding a good dose of texture. The adjacent master bath is a relaxing hideaway that feels like more than a bathroom, with lively touches such as the 1930s Gottardo Piazzoni painting and the 1950s light fixture over the soaking tub.

One of my favorite spaces in this home is what I call the playroom—it's a little oasis, a vacation behind a door. I wanted to use a nostalgic, comforting hue for the walls, so I chose this green paint I've been drawn to for years—it's a similar color to one that California's Bauer Pottery used in the 1950s for their glazes. It has a memory sense to it—while it's an intense color, it's also inherently soothing, because it's a throwback to calmer times. So the mood in this room isn't overly serious, a few key pieces provide levity, including the sculptural wood chair and the antique Italian lamps. I love mixing vintage pieces into every interior—it's necessary for every home to have a sense of history. Each item has to be well considered—if a room is too heavy on antiques, or too heavy on contemporary pieces, it tips the balance. The carefully combined blend gave this brand-new house its aura of timelessness, while maintaining my design edict to always leave room for evolution and change.

OPPOSITE: A paisley wallcovering in the dining room goes modern, thanks to its large-scale pattern repeat. The blue palette paired with natural finishes creates a calming atmosphere for guests.
FOLLOWING PAGES: Purchasing art with personal meaning, be it vintage finds or highly collectible pieces—rather than store-bought "filler" art, which is so easy to spot—is key to creating an original space.

The magic word
in any vignette
is *curation.*
When you pare
back your
belongings to what
truly matters, you
liberate your senses—and
enhance your life.

In the master bedroom, a tucked-away writing nook is a beautiful reminder to create simple yet striking vignettes throughout your home. The hand-painted wallpaper with a troweled effect brings the room's high vaulted ceilings down to earth.

Sculptural furniture and estate-sale
lamps turned this bonus room
into a playroom that's a marked
departure from the rest of the home.

Lofty Goals

Designing for a single man is markedly different from designing for a couple or a single woman—men often have a different list of priorities. Not only are there typically more and larger televisions (no joke), but the comfort level of the furniture and the functionality of the home also often take priority over the aesthetic. Men entertain differently, too, so it's a wildly different set of bells and whistles in the common areas.

When your penthouse overlooks a panoramic view of downtown L.A.'s urban skyline, you want to show it off. My client sought interiors that are fuss-free and stripped-down—he wanted a minimized color palette and a raw, utilitarian vibe. But as he is drawn to L.A.'s seemingly omnipresent blue sky, he asked me to bring all the varying shades of it inside as accents. So while the overall base palette is a rugged mix of grays and wood grains, different blues—azure, lapis, and indigo—supply great effect.

Fixtures and furniture with industrial flavor—sculptural pieces that hew masculine and functional—add to the loft vibe. Nothing is staged or overdecorated—it's effortless. In the dining area, the steel table was made from the reclaimed parts of an old bridge. Above it, the faceted-bronze chandelier casts a filtered, flattering light. And speaking of functionality: in the screening room that doubles as a spare bedroom, a covert Murphy bed hides in a custom-designed wall unit. It may only be used once a year, but it's at the ready for occasional guests.

Because this is my client's weekend home, there isn't much personal clutter. What remains is a carefully edited mix of books, textures, and objets that are lovely, memory-filled places for the eye to land. It's the same concept as a movie director zooming in on a particular part of a scene: if an object is important to your story, make it a focal point.

The media room's custom wall unit has a secret: the table folds down and transforms into a Murphy bed for guests. The 1970s lamps on either side are lit from within, with a disco effect.

Faceted-bronze chandeliers and a dining room table made from the upcycled parts of a former steel bridge set a masculine tone in this bachelor pad loft that overlooks downtown Los Angeles.

If you're blessed with a commanding view, own it.

Select furniture with strong architectural silhouettes to exalt a geometric skyline beyond.

OPPOSITE: Cool grays and occasional blues in a variety of angular textures formed the base color palette for an industrial feel. FOLLOWING PAGES: A high/low mix of modern pieces surround the fire pit on the terrace for entertaining; muted wood furniture softens the steel gray scheme. Every furniture piece is sculptural to hold its own against the dynamics of the architectural cityscape beyond the terrace.

Expansive wall mirrors give the illusion of an even larger space in the open kitchen and dining area. With sapphire blue tiles in 1970s-era shapes, the wraparound kitchen-island peninsula becomes its own destination. A literally open bar connotes that this home has a laid-back, party-ready atmosphere.

An artisan-made blanket of chunky crocheted wool is the focal point of the bedroom. Metallic pendant lights hung above the bedside tables allow you to use the entire tabletops for books, objets, and a nightcap. The upholstered walls absorb sound and also form a nice contrast against the angular abstract painting.

Rustic/Modern

When my clients, a young couple with three sons, were building this Lake Tahoe getaway home, they asked me to design interiors that looked appropriate to the location, yet still had their own distinctive voice. To stay far away from the usual Tahoe design tropes, materials and furniture are in line with the postcard-picturesque surroundings yet take the interiors to a different level.

Because this was their first time building a home from the ground up, trust was even more important to our relationship than normal, and our connection played a huge part in the beautiful outcome. Sometimes projects can become overwhelming for people, and that's when the concept of the big picture really comes into play. I constantly reiterate what the end goal is—and that it will all be worth it. It helped that this client had an innate sense of how function and style can work together. She was very in tune with her family's needs, and how they wanted to live.

We kicked off the project with a trip to Paris to scour the flea markets, where we unearthed all manner of interesting finds to use as decorative starting points. Take the immense antique wooden key that hangs above the custom bench I designed in the entryway: it's a surprising relic to have hung in a foyer, and it announces from the minute you enter the house that this is no typical rustic California cabin. Many of the fixtures are former Parisian streetlamps and lanterns, which I reworked into eye-catching pendants that put on an optic show.

The family is very environmentally conscious, something I kept top of mind with every single decision. We sourced the granite stones for the towering fireplace locally. Reclaimed barn siding is utilized throughout the home, on walls and even ceilings, to imbue the newly built rooms with storied history; it is often arranged in unorthodox

OPPOSITE: A colossal antique key purchased in Paris presides over the foyer, with a Shaker-inspired custom bench and a door that echoes the reclaimed-wood pattern used on the dining room wall.
FOLLOWING PAGES: Natural materials—locally sourced granite, reclaimed wood, and leather and linen upholstery—give the home an earthy aesthetic that's perfectly in keeping with its milieu.

In a setting like this, the view itself is the artwork—there's little need to invest in paintings with an overlook like Lake Tahoe. FOLLOWING PAGES: Reclaimed barn siding becomes modern in the dining room when placed in an angular pattern reminiscent of chevron stripes. The pendants were repurposed from antique Parisian streetlights; the intricate 1970s wall sculpture by Curtis Jeré pops against the angular wood wall.

Open-beam ceilings add architectural integrity to the kitchen and are accented by shimmering custom pendant lights over the island.

ABOVE: Hints of modernity, such as this colorful painting at the end of a long hallway, are vital in a home that utilizes reclaimed wood, lest it become a cliché.

OPPOSITE: A collection of vintage brass longhorn heads lends Wild West street cred to the game room, while refined printed linen fabrics keep the look homespun.

Reclaimed and indigenous elements can still be modern when used sparingly. Beauty comes in combinations and juxtapositions.

ways—such as in the dining room, where a chevron-like pattern forms an intricate backdrop for a 1970s metal wall sculpture. Natural upholstery materials, like leather, linen, and wool, suit the eco-friendly agenda. Every element of the home speaks to its setting, even in the most function-driven spaces; the master bath has granite walls and an industrial-looking steel-and-glass shower enclosure that mimics an old factory window, a modernist version of Tahoe chic. Most of the rooms have open-beam ceilings, which impart architectural integrity with a lakeside sensibility. I consider ceilings the fifth wall—as one of the largest surfaces in a space, they deserve attention.

Like most getaways, the view is the artwork in this home. To maximize the lakefront panorama in the home's main living room, glimmering custom light fixtures don't obstruct the windows—they merely add a dose of sculptural interest. The colors—all muted grays and browns—keep the focus on the brilliant blues and greens beyond the glass. I used the same tack in the kitchen, opting for clear custom light fixtures that would complement the shimmering lakeside scene.

In the end, even though this is a vacation house, it's still *home*. Getaways can't be impersonal and cold. Everything should have a sense of place and purpose so it always seems familiar and supportive, even with the adventurous wilds of a classic California vacationland right outside the door.

OPPOSITE: Suedes and natural linens cozy up the limestone-walled master bedroom. Ceramic elements provide a sense of home that's especially essential in a vacation house. FOLLOWING PAGES, LEFT: A shower enclosure made to look like steel factory windows is in line with the rugged appearance of the master bathroom. FOLLOWING PAGES, RIGHT: Stone walls that line the length of the bathroom wall create a feeling of storied permanence.

OPPOSITE: Each of the couple's sons has his own faucet at an antique-look bathroom sink. Subway-tile walls and shiplap-effect cabinetry and medicine cabinets radiate timeless, vintage cool. ABOVE: Custom-made trundle beds for the family's three boys translate to a cheerful summer-camp vibe; blue striped fabrics, faux-fur beanbag chairs, and antler chandeliers say *bunk room*. FOLLOWING PAGES: Even in a grand vacation home, it's important to keep things from becoming ostentatious. This chic bedroom is the quintessential example of comfort.

Personal Style

My design philosophy is to live life beautifully and to the fullest, and to always surround yourself with things that make you happy. I favor classic design with a definite edge, and an emphasis on vintage and custom elements. Comfort and livability—with a touch of glamour, always!—are also key to my aesthetic. My personal style is constantly evolving, and my own homes are my design laboratories.

t

here is a bit of choreography to my rooms in the way things are placed and how you move through them, which is fitting, given my past life as a choreographer. Doing my own staging, wardrobe, art direction, and set design honed my ability to visualize the big picture without getting mired in the everyday.

Choreography and interior design are cut from the same exquisite cloth, so the transition was seamless. They are both made up of multiple moving parts that need to flow effortlessly into one beautiful and cohesive result. My primary focus when designing a room is movement—from the path your eye takes, to the physicality of your body in motion, to the life a room takes on when filled with people. Movement is a vital element of decor—the unseen layer that connects a space—and it's all akin to choreography. A house should never really be considered finished or complete, it should be in continual motion, alive with you.

When I moved into this 1930 Spanish Colonial house in L.A.'s Miracle Mile North neighborhood, I did a few detail-oriented basics: I had the hardware stripped down to its original antiqued-brass finish, refinished the oak floors, and redesigned the fireplace for a modern take that was still suited to a Spanish bungalow's architecture. But since I wasn't on a schedule, I just did what felt natural and let things happen organically. Making my house my home is a passion for me, but there are times when I am my own worst client! I am last on the list of importance; there were so many times I'd see an amazing, beautiful piece, but instinctively think of a specific client before myself. But I'm so glad I took my time. The accumulation of your belongings is one way of telling the story of your life. As you get older, possessions take on more meaning;

OPPOSITE: I fell in love with this still-life painting because it looks so realistic—like objects sitting on a mantel. It's now a visual play above my marble mantel and provides great depth of field. The sconces were custom designed around vintage glass. FOLLOWING PAGES: The living room isn't overly designed, but rather a collection of beloved things I've acquired over the years that speak to my design aesthetic. In my own home, I avoid conventional furniture arrangements in favor of placing each piece the way I actually use it.

Living artfully is important to me. Collecting and editing have to go hand in hand.

you fall in love with certain objects. It's as if they're old friends. All the pieces come together to make a house feel like home, and they're embedded in your memory of what *home* means. So if something has personal meaning to you, even if it seems like an outlier aesthetically, try to find a way to work it into your design story.

As an Aries, I'm a trailblazer—a little bit fearless. I won't let anyone tell me I can't do something; I just make it work. When I first became a designer, there were no big budgets, so I thought, What can I bring to the table that is spectacular? The answer was my creativity. I have never had any formal design training, but I learned to trust my instincts. At the end of the day, I'm the only person who can call myself successful. Nobody else can define that for me. It sounds cliché, but it's true—and it's true when it comes to the design of your home as well. It's *your* creation. Like life itself, your personal style is constantly evolving, but certain design trademarks must remain: visually inspiring elements, living artistically, in comfort with your own version of glamour at every turn.

OPPOSITE: I've always been enamored with pottery for the individuality of it—no two pieces are alike. FOLLOWING PAGES: I selected a monochromatic color palette for my living room. Because the window treatments blend with the walls and even the grass cloth on the ceiling, nothing stands out, and yet there's so much depth of color found in the varying textures.

OPPOSITE: Arranging vintage and contemporary ceramics in a singular hue and similar shape makes them more impactful. ABOVE: Everything needs to be curated, including functional office supplies. Even the simplest things can take on a level of personal glamour. FOLLOWING PAGES, LEFT: My Shiba Inu, Beck, lounging on a chaise I designed for my collection for A. Rudin. The table was a thrift-store find; I upholstered the top in suede. FOLLOWING PAGES, RIGHT: I love abstract paintings; this grouping is composed primarily of pieces by Laura Lancaster, a London artist. I purchased the desk years ago at a Paris flea market and have had it ever since. Vignettes are so important; there should be a beautiful little design story wherever you cast your eye.

ABOVE: A collection of ceramic art pieces by Adam Silverman, my favorite contemporary potter. OPPOSITE: Chairs from my collection for A. Rudin atop a rug by Kyle Bunting—I love the mix! The art piece is a portrait made entirely of paint chips by Peter Combe.

Making bold design choices has been instrumental in my design evolution. We shape our homes, and they shape us.

OPPOSITE: My den is purposefully eclectic and funky, with a real sense of home, thanks to its mass assemblage of objects and paintings I've collected over the years that work organically together. This vintage table has a glazed ceramic top—an earthy note that is a nice counterbalance to the sofa I designed and upholstered in an Hermès fabric. A tiny bit of extravagance that makes me smile! FOLLOWING PAGES: A light fixture I had custom made of ceramic pieces by Los Angeles potter Heather Levine holds court over the room.

ABOVE: I'm drawn to a classic kitchen. I considered ripping everything out of this circa-1930s one, but embraced it instead in keeping with the old-Hollywood bungalow aesthetic and did modest renovations. OPPOSITE: I couldn't resist adding slightly creepy-yet-amazing Fornasetti wallpaper in the breakfast nook. The built-in cabinetry is original; interesting architecture should be championed whenever possible, rather than made modern for the sake of being modern. The chairs are by Roy McMakin, repurposed in high gloss Farrow & Ball paint in the color Down Pipe.

A trio from my collection of vintage Bauer bowls set above the farmhouse sink. The countertops are black granite.

The essence of style is confidence. Keep things original and meaningful to achieve real personal glamour.

OPPOSITE: The rug, one of my designs—called Brushstroke—for my collection for Mansour Modern, inspired the color palette in my bedroom. I matched the curtain fabric to the walls exactly for continuity. I custom designed the wall sconces because I wanted something sculptural, yet with an animated sense of humor. FOLLOWING PAGES, LEFT: I wanted my own bedroom to be an exercise in design restraint. The masculine color palette includes cerused-black oak bedside tables and teal-gray walls with brass accents. FOLLOWING PAGES, RIGHT: A vintage abstract painting takes the place of an extravagant headboard.

ABOVE: I indulgently renovated my bathroom with Calacatta tiles, brass inlay, and distressed antique limestone floors, tied together with unlacquered brass accents. It's become my favorite room in the house. OPPOSITE: A commanding freestanding bathtub with a burnished-nickel exterior and brass fittings by Waterworks were the starting point for the room's design. The photography in my bathroom is by my friend David Rogers. Danish glass pieces are by Holmegaard. Wall sconces are by Apparatus.

ABOVE AND OPPOSITE: I designed my closet to look like a proper gentleman's dressing room, tailoring the space to be clean and organized. Almost everything is tucked into tidy drawers or behind mirrored closet doors. Dream closet realized.

Cheers!

There are so many people who have helped shape me into the man and designer I am today. This book is a celebration of creativity, and it could not have happened alone.

THANK YOU / To Rich Pedine, for standing by me and guiding me through literally everything, always; Jill Cohen, for recognizing potential and cultivating it beautifully; Doug Turshen, Steve Turner, Kathleen Jayes, and Charles Miers, for making this happen so creatively and seamlessly; and Kathryn O'Shea-Evans, for tirelessly listening, having my voice, and going on this journey with me. I appreciate you more than I can express. Thank you Grey Crawford for lending me your talents as a photographer and always finding La Luce, as well as Laura Hull, Susan Gilmore, Tim Street-Porter, and Stephen Buskin for your beautiful images.

THANK YOU / To all of the clients who have invited me into their lives: I would not be celebrating my work without you. To Eleanor Mondale, my first real design client and a wonderful friend; Tom Boule, for seeing me as a designer; Jen "Lady" Messer, for picking me up, dusting me off, and making me earn it . . . . several times; Josh Greenberg, for all the opportunities; Claudia and Barry Poznick, for love, friendship, and Larb; Ryan Seacrest, for giving me a chance; Khloé Kardashian, for trusting me; Kris Jenner, for kicking me up a notch; Kourtney Kardashian, for collaborating with me; Sarah and Jason Dilullo, for taking me to the next level; Tyson and Kimberly Chandler, for having such great taste; Joe and Kathi Costello, for going on the journey; and Alan and Emily Feit, for believing in me. Thank you, Kaley Cuoco, for light, positivity, encouragement, and being the perfect client always!

My design career has taken several twists and turns, including working with many extremely talented friends and mentors who once danced with me while I was a choreographer or who are a big part of the dance community. Thanks to Luca Tommassini, Jamie King, Carrie Ann Inaba, Joe Tremaine, Mandy Moore, and Brian Freidman—to name a few. The creative process is something that evolves with you, and working with other visionaries has been a special part of my life both as a choreographer and an interior designer.

THANK YOU / To the people who have worked with me throughout my design career and never let me down: Christina Chapin, Dan Cordova, Jennifer Kim, Laura Roberts, John McHenry, Pia Diona, and Nadia Trevino to name a few. Renee Fontana, my flower goddess, and Patty Maldonado, for always telling me I'm rich; to the very generous people who have trusted me and collaborated with me on my foray into product design: Ralph and Spencer Rudin, Aaron Kirsch, Benjamin Solemani, Jamie Beckwith, Jane Sieberts, and Kim Muroff; and to the showrooms, artisans, contractors, and behind-the-scenes people who see my visions and help make things possible—I thank you.

LAST THANKS / To my family, for loving me unconditionally; my sister Julie, for constant support; Marene Babula, my forever pickle girl; Tanya Zabin, for never-ending enthusiasm; Karen Mandel, for laughs and lifelong friendship; Suzie Hardy, the best poopoohead ever; and Annette English, for patience and guidance.

To Raj Kapoor, for admiring my talent and putting me on a pedestal I want to live up to . . . . always. I love you and greatly admire *your* talent and aspire to have your work ethic. I'm so proud of you.

And to Jessica Tarazona, my rock. Your constant dedication and devotion is the most powerful support I have known, in design and in life. I love and appreciate you more than you know.

First published in the United States of America in 2019
by Rizzoli International Publications, Inc.
300 Park Avenue South
New York, NY 10010
www.rizzoliusa.com

Photography by Grey Crawford except for pages:
4, 5: Susan Gilmore
11, 223: Stephen Buskin
129: Tim Street-Porter
158-173: Laura Hull

2019 2020 2021 2022 / 10 9 8 7 6 5 4 3 2 1

Distributed in the U.S. trade by Random House, New York

Designed by Doug Turshen with Steve Turner

Printed in China

ISBN-13: 978-0-8478-6632-8

Library of Congress Catalog Control Number: 2018959591

Cézanne
a life
Alex
Danchev